It was a delight to be sent an account of a childhood beginning in the very house where this little book is now published. The teacher ringing her curfew bell across the "Dom" to send Scarthin children to bed, Billie Mee the blacksmith hammering in the Market Place, the wheelwright, the dynasties of butchers, "Long John" Marsden-Smedley – and the Judgment Tree – are just some of the local legends described from memory here. Though much has changed, all generations will agree that Cromford has remained a most wonderful village in which to grow up – and personally I am most fortunate to have found here in Scarthin such a magical place in which to live and work.

David Mitchell
Scarthin Books

Eddie and mother Ethel c 1919.

Around
CROMFORD DAM

Growing up in Scarthin and Cromford between the Wars

by ALFRED EDWARD GEORGE ALLSOP

Scarthin Books, Cromford, Derbyshire

2005

*Cromford Cricket Club, some time in the 1930's (back row from left Cyril Kidd,
Harry Noble and George Rollinson; front row in the middle
Mr Borling [Captain], Ray Buxton, Mr Ditchfield).*

ACKNOWLEDGEMENTS

The drawings and personal photographs reproduced are from the author's collection.
Thanks to Janet Kirk for providing other illustrations
and to Jean Howsley for the amazing list of businesses.

Published 2005 by Scarthin Books, Cromford, Derbyshire.

© Alfred Edward George Allsop

Cover Photograph © David Mitchell, 2005

ISBN 1 900446 08 1

CONTENTS

Eddie (on the right) with cousins Jean and Russell.

CHAPTER ONE

SCARTHIN HOUSE

Should I write about the house I used to live in? The house is still there; in fact the road it stands on is called Scarthin. The dwelling appears superficially at least to have changed very little. I have no doubt that the present owner would be quite happy to show me around, but then it would lose so much of its mystique. Would my earliest, short, largely unconnected memories be enhanced? Would those with whom it was peopled seem any more real? I doubt it. After all, I was only seven when we left. I do not suppose that the actual move affected me very much. I think that on that day I went to school as usual to be met after school was over and taken to our new home.

I was born in Scarthin House a few months before the end of the First World War. I understand that my coming was not easy, that Mother 'had a hard time'. I just do not know if Dad was able to have leave from the Royal Flying Corps to be with her. I hope so. Grandpa Roworth lived with us then. Did he own the house? It seems likely that he could have bought the house when he retired from his grocery business in Chesterfield. Grandma Roworth, who died in 1917, is buried in Cromford cemetery.

The family Roworth were staunch Methodist, active in the Primitive Methodist organisation. Grandpa was a local preacher and it was here in the little chapel at the top of Tap Road that I was christened by him. The chapel is still recognisable, a tall black building bearing a little board indicating that it was once an offshoot, a representation of the 'Prims' in Cromford.

Dad was in business in Scarthin when I was little. He had set up to deal in second-hand furniture, some of which he bought in from the auction sales conducted by Wheatcrofts of Matlock. With any item needing repair he would do what was required and finish off the work by varnishing and polishing. He would also undertake small jobs that a joiner could do in the homes of his customers. Did the business exist as I was to know it before he joined the RFC? He was originally apprenticed as a cabinetmaker to Eyre's of Chesterfield. I never heard him state that he had been employed by anyone else.

Scarthin House was quite an impressive building with six large windows on the upper floors built over a shop, all of good sandstone. At the back of the shop was a closed-in staircase which gave access to the living accommodation above. The formal entrance to this was by a door at the side of the building, partway up a long flight of stone steps that climbed higher and higher up the hillside of Scarthin Nick. The door opened into the hall. On the right hand a further door opened to quite a large kitchen with open beams. I can only remember that the main light was from a large window looking out on to a partially covered stone paved yard with a few steps up to the garden. The main back wall built into the hillside was without a window, but I may be wrong about this.

The way to the garden was through the scullery. The garden itself was entirely overlooked by a row of cottages built behind a high stone wall. There was what might have been a lawn fringed with rockeries. I distinctly remember huge ferns, blue flag irises and little else.

Mother was friendly with one of the families living above us. We exchanged visits. They had two teenage girls. One day when I was there I was absolutely fascinated to watch oatcakes being made on a plate over the kitchen range. Were the oatcakes sooty I wondered? The little family emigrated to New Zealand around 1923. I wonder what happened to them.

Mother disliked the open beams in the kitchen and so persuaded Dad to board them in with plywood. I suppose the ceiling might then have been whitewashed or even papered.

To the left of the entrance hall was a small partitioned-off enclosure of wood panelling and glass, surmounted by an elaborately cut heading with coloured glass panels; there was also pink paper attachments. What ever could they have been?

We referred to this room as the study. In its day, once the door was closed, it must have been a quiet haven, cut off from the endless comings and goings of an extended family. The only object that interested me was an old treadle sewing machine which unfortunately had been rendered useless as Aunty Lily was said to have tried to lubricate it with Oil of Linseed!

Beyond the study there were two rooms opening on to the front of the house. The smaller could have been a storeroom; it just did not make any impression on me. The larger, our drawing room, with its two windows, afforded beautiful views. In the near foreground, the Prom, with its bronze soldier on the War Memorial looking into the distance, the Cromford Dam with its waterwheel and millrace, and behind, all the high hills of the Moor below Black Rocks. From our elevated viewpoint we could follow all the passers-by in the street below.

The furniture in what was our drawing room included a large table and sideboard with matching upright chairs. (Which reminds me that the Doctor had suggested that I should be given cod liver oil. However, as it was difficult to persuade me that it was good for me, cod liver oil and malt was provided. I quite enjoyed this medicine which was left conveniently on the sideboard. I helped myself quite liberally to the extent that I came out in spots.) An old photograph depicts that this room had a heavy wallpaper and a cast-iron

Lounge in Scarthin House c. 1910 – now the Art Room; the cupboard and bookcase are still there.

9

fireplace with tile surrounds. The overmantle, supporting a large mirror, was draped with a dark embroided cloth. In an alcove was a china cabinet with bookshelves underneath.

Mother and Dad on Sunday afternoons used to go to the chapel next door where they had informal meetings which included some hymn singing which Dad accompanied on the organ. To pass the time I would lay the table for tea. It was remarked that I always put out jam, marmalade and treacle. Plenty of choice!

I am not likely to forget, when coming home from school one day, I followed the other kids onto Water Lane where a gate gave access to the Dam. Of course I was forbidden to go there, but Mother saw me, opened the window and shouted. For the first and only time she walloped me with a strip of wood from Dad's workshop.

There were I believe four bedrooms, one large and one small, matching in size the reception rooms below. Mother and Dad had the front room; I had a small one at the back. The other which had become a boxroom was, when cousins Jean and Russell came to stay, our playground and it was there that I discovered some of the differences between girls and boys. There was a bathroom, but I have no recollection of being bathed in there.

All this extensive household called for a deal of work. Fortunately we had Mrs Shaw who lived nearby. I can see her now washing the lino at the top of the stairs and at the same time keeping an eye on me. There were two boys in her family, the eldest, Eric, had taught himself to play the squeeze box (accordion). He was a big ginger-haired lad who eventually developed a good bass voice and was much in demand for local concert parties. The younger boy, Jim, was a particular friend of mine. We played together on the Prom, but I could not have him in the house, although I was always welcome in his home.

I had a Noah's Ark with wooden animals of which I was very fond. Sadly I left it out in the rain, the printed paper animals peeled off, the rain softened the glue in the Ark so that too was lost. Dad was cross. My favourite toy was a red wooden engine that he made for me. I could sit on it and push it along with my feet, but when the wheels came off it was Grandpa who repaired it.

Another friend, Jack, lived in a little cottage high up on the hill behind us. His father was a signalman who worked the Cromford box. He took us there once to watch him at work, pulling the levers that moved the points and signals whilst all the time listening to bells. His cottage was completely bounded by a brick wall, just high enough to see over. It was here in this tiny yard that we played together. Jack's mother would not allow him to come down to the Prom for games with the rest of us. It seems that I was considered a suitable playmate. He was already playing their piano, an instrument that was dreadfully out of tune. I do not know whether he had lessons, but included in his repertoire was the Blue Danube Waltz. I wonder if here lies the root of my dislike of this particular piece of music? Small beginnings for Jack, but he would one day be commissioned into the Royal Air Force where he formed a dance band on his station.

What a wonderful playground the Prom made for us, bounded as it was with high iron railings that kept us safe from the deep water of the Dam. With the exception of small ball games we amused ourselves with endless skipping, jumping, running until we were dropping with fatigue, hot, dirty but happy. Then there was always something happening in and around the pond. Occasionally men would take out a boat and punt themselves around, but for what purpose? We could watch the swans scrapping with Ma Pidcock's ducks. There were always dragonflies, and then inexplicable spots of dampness – we said it must be the pissy-ants! In the autumn, snowstorms of airborne seeds floated across from the weed-filled banks – angels we called them.

I do not remember the older boys interfering with our games. Perhaps they had been given work to do to earn a few pennies.

There was very little traffic along the road, almost all horsedrawn. The milkman would stop at the bottom of our steps to carry a pail of milk to our door from which he would fill Mother's jug and fill a cup for me if I was there. The coalman, too, carried bags to us. There must have been a coal-hole or some such; he would never have been allowed to come through the hall. A pony and trap, driven by one of the Arkwrights would stop by, often loaded with flowers. It seemed that all our food shopping was done locally, anything we needed was available in the Market Place.

Again I wonder who built the house there, surrounded as it was

11

Around Cromford Dam

by small dwellings rising row upon row up the steep hillsides, houses, hovels really, without sanitation and reached only by endless worn steps. In recent years many of them have been demolished, some to be replaced by odd pink sandstone buildings. After we left, the house passed to a Mr Fletcher with two girls, Kathleen and Lorna, a man who had ambitions to become a local councillor. The Dam was heavily silted, perhaps it smelled. Whether Mr Fletcher was one of those who would like to have had it filled in as some advocated, I don't know, but he had painted hand bills which proclaimed "Vote for Fletcher and get rid of the Dam nuisance" The slogan was misinterpreted by some who in any case regarded it as unseemly. Anyway his candidature failed.

Two dear old ladies, Miss Tomlinson, a Sunday School teacher, and Mrs Kirk set up a milliner's there that lasted for a few years until the former died. From then on there is a large gap in my history of Scarthin House, but it now boasts a huge sign "The Scarthin Bookshop" together with floodlights disfiguring the beautiful stonework. The chapel next door was gutted years ago to make a machine shop. Only the War Memorial, first placed there after World War I, survives, but now has additional names added to mark World War II. But after so many years and pressure applied by the Arkwright Preservation Society the Dam has been cleared. Moorhens, dippers, ducks are returning after the upheaval, the swans have their own island to nest in; all is well in their little world.

The road is no longer a background for horse drawn vehicles; in fact there are a few cars parked on the side leaving just sufficient carriageway to operate a oneway street system between the Market Place and Water Lane. Part of the wall of the Promenade collapsed fairly recently, no doubt as a result of vibration caused by the traffic.

It is well that Scarthin is still a narrow street. Across the Dam, Water Lane has become the highway into Via Gellia, a road built for the carriages of the Gells of Hopton Hall. Cromford Hill which climbs steeply towards Wirksworth carries endless loads of limestone from the Middleton Mine. The rows of cottages built by Sir Richard Arkwright for his workers are now protected by great steel barriers; accidents are frequent. The Market Place is little more now than a road junction serving the A6 trunk road.

CHAPTER TWO

CHILDHOOD DAYS IN CROMFORD

Marbles on the 'Dom'.

In the Spring we had several street games scarcely heard of nowadays, e.g. bowling. In this game a light wooden ring, guided by a stick, was chased at great speed. Unfortunately the bowl could run away and get broken. There was a posh job, a steel ring with a steel rod attached, which when pursued gave a most satisfactory noise on the cobbled streets.

Whip and Top was a very old game. The top, a roughly conical shaped piece of wood with grooves, was produced on a lathe. The whip had a wooden handle with a lash made of string, the latter to be wound round the top. To operate it the top was held under the heel and the string was pulled away, hopefully causing the top to spin. Then the top was vigorously whipped to continue the spinning. With skill the top could be made to bound through the air.

Marbles was another favourite; coloured marbles made of clay were the norm. Often glass marbles were included in the play with a scale of value based on one for a clay marble and ten for a glass specimen. Oddly enough the source of this little glass sphere was a pop bottle with a pinched neck, the marble under the gas pressure in the bottle effectively sealed the bottle. There were a few large marbles available. I was given one, a beautiful specimen of the glass-workers art as big as a gob-stopper; on scale of value worth twenty five. I took it out to play and lost it in less time than it takes to tell. I did not

13

understand the rules of the game then and I have to admit that I still don't know. But my enemy knew.

Poor Stanley, he is dead now, but he and I fought many times. One bout I well remember was when he managed to tuck my head under his arm and then proceeded to thump my nose with his free hand.

To return to marbles, we almost always played on the Promenade fronting the Scarthin Dam, the "Dom" as it was really known. There was a hole in the tarmacadam which made a super spot to aim for, which reminds me of scooters. I had an iron model with small wheels. I loved that scooter, perhaps less well when I steered myself right into that same marble hole. I was projected over the top in the exact way horse and rider part company in the Grand National.

Another game we played and associated with Whitsuntide and Spring was battledore and shuttlecock which I understand still survives. Everyone skipped and there were endless round games such as 'Piggy in the Middle', the piggy being chosen by elimination whilst all the kids chanted Eenie Meenie Miney Mo or some such. Because silent films had given us the vision of the Wild West of America we fought as Cowboys and Indians.

Stanley again comes to mind. He was the youngest of the Pidcocks, with four brothers and three sisters. I think, but I am not quite sure, their father had been lost in the Great War. [It was actually an uncle who was killed in the war, their father died about 1924 ... DJM.] They were indeed a tough lot. Cromford Dam was very neglected. Originally it had served the brewery which in Cromford was represented by the Brewery. The dam was becoming heavily silted actually forming a dry weedy bank under the promenade wall. This was known as Pickott's Isle. Mrs Pidcock had managed to keep a few hens and ducks there. Truly a pioneer in the development of wild places. Now there is actually a building on the site, a summer house. In 1997–8 the Dom had a clean-up to meet the standards of a Heritage Village in keeping with the requirements of the Sir Richard Arkwright Preservation Society, but Pickott's Isle remains. Will it have to be noted in the latest survey map?

When winter came, there was always snow, or so it seemed.

14

Snowballing was for us all, not without its hazards. We sledged down Penny Ford in Mee's field. He was wonderfully tolerant because the more reckless ended up in his garden. I had a super sledge, made for me by Dad, joiner-made in fact. He had runners especially made by Billy Mee the blacksmith with round edges, when every boy knew that runners should be flat. No blacksmith laboured over these. They came from the strips salvaged from an old iron bedstead. For speed, flats were the goods. Some of the more daring sledged down Cromford Hill and were said to have overtaken Watt's buses – not really very surprising. Buses on that hill crawled down, as did all the very limited traffic plying from Wirksworth to Cromford.

We lived on Cromford Hill for a short time after leaving Scarthin. The cottage was one of Arkwright's built to accommodate the workers in his mills. These houses were one room wide; there was the living room and at the back of the house was the kitchen. The staircase led out of the living room to two bedrooms, one behind the other. There was no water supply – water was available across the road from a tap. In winter, although I do not remember the tap ever freezing, the splashing produced dangerous ice round about. No water, therefore there was no lavatory within the house. The 'place' was up the garden and was of the most primitive. At the back of the

Cromford Hill on Carnival Day (much more recently: Janet Batterley, Carnival Queen 1954).

15

little building was a shutter, or something, permitting the accumulated offerings to be dug out and then dug into the garden. Dad was not much interested in gardening and so for a short time the garden was my playground. With the help of my friend Bob Morse, we dug a huge hole. Imagine our dismay when we found that our lovely hole had been enlarged and the contents of the bog had been thrown into it. However, I suppose we moved up a peg in the social scale by having a portable pan put in which could be emptied by the night soil operative who <u>did</u> come by night with his horse and cart.

Practically everything came or went by horse and cart. Milk was collected in a jug straight from the churn. Palin's of Wirksworth delivered fruit and vegetables. When he stopped some of the kids would shout "Any busdie apples Mr Palin?" Anyone fortunate to have a whole apple to eat would be entreated to "Save us t'core". Coal was delivered at a shilling a bag. It came in by canal. Wheatcroft was the agent who had an unloading wharf at the end of the Cromford Cut.

Mending the road on Cromford Hill was a great event. A steamroller would grind its way up the hill tearing out the old limestone surface. This was followed by wetting and then a good deal of rolling. During this process everything and everybody living on the hill was enveloped in dust and mud. In later years, of course, tarmacadam was introduced, but in those days hill surfaces were designed for the horse.

It was about this time that the first motor buses came to travel between Cromford and Matlock. One was a blue bus run by Hands and the other a yellow favoured by a competitor, Furness. These were open top wagons following in design the earlier horse drawn charabancs. It was a great day when double deckers, open topped, similar to the horse-drawn trams, came into service. Now it was necessary for a conductor to collect the fares. Paying must have been a bit of a joke which led to the fable of hearing the conductor and driver sharing out the pennies. "One for me, one for you and one for old Furness".

Marvellously a bus service was established between Matlock and Wirksworth, the owner, Watts. George Elliott, in writing a best seller

of its period in 1859 – '*Adam Bede*' – gave her characters some Derbyshire connections. Watts named his first little bus Adam Bede, a black, sit up and beg box, looking not unlike the Model T Ford with springs similar to those of horse carriages. Later editions he named Seth Bede and Diana Morris so perpetuating the names. In Cromford there is a Bedehouse Lane.

To return to Scarthin House. Remarkably the shop and house have been preserved in their original condition [hidden behind the books … DJM]. Dad had a furniture business which, with repair work and small joinery jobs, gave us a living. He used to attend sales conducted at the Mart in Matlock by Wheatcroft. One wonderful day he brought home three organs, one a street organ and another a smaller instrument for home entertainment which he put in the shop window where I turned the handle to the envy of the kids who gathered around to watch and listen.

Next door was a non-conformist chapel where Dad played the organ on Sunday afternoon at the 'P.S.A.' (which I know now was "Pleasant Sunday Afternoons".)

Beyond again was a shop selling stationery kept by Tossie Smith, whose husband had a little printing works producing hand bills and advertisements, programmes and what-have-you. Because his works was tucked away in his garden, we could not resist climbing the wall to see what he was doing only to be chased off.

Mother often sent me on errands to Britlands the grocer. The shop was only a cottage with a little shop window displaying sweets. One of my errands was for treacle for which I carried a stone jar. Mr Britland would take the jar and place it under a black iron machine mounted on the counter, pull a lever and out would come a lovely brown stream of treacle. When Mother was bread-making my errand would be for yeast which she always called 'balm' which I nibbled on the way home. Similarly I could not help sipping the vinegar from a jug. Except for tinned food, practically all goods arrived in the shop in bulk to be weighed out, packed in sturdy brown paper. Butter was in tubs, flour in bags, tea in lead-lined chests which could be bought for a shilling to carry safely precious glasses and china for a flitting (remove).

Marsden's the chemist I sometimes visited. Shelves reached the

Shoe-shop and Chemist's in Edwardian days.

ceiling, all lined with strange looking bottles, the counters with little drawers all marked in gold leaf. In the window were huge containers filled with brightly coloured liquids. Perhaps I had been sent to collect a bottle of medicine. Mr Marsden always wrapped the bottle in white paper, then sealed the flap with sealing wax melted by a fearsome machine that produced a crackling discharge of electricity. Dad went often to the shop. He used to study the display of Parkinson's pills – "Pink Pills for Poorly People" we used to call them. Each packet made remarkable claims for treatment of an amazing variety of complaints. He sampled a good lot of them. Unfortunately for me he would insist on dosing me with camomile flowers stewed on the hob overnight. Sometimes I would be persuaded to drink a concoction of boiled liquorice powder with spanish juice simmered in it. Well despite all I am still around.

Influenza was a regular hazard. I fear sometimes that I was attended to as if I was a machine needing oiling. The remedy for a sore throat was to swallow a large spoonful of butter decorated with sugar. Sweating had to be forced. I was placed in the dolly tub up to my neck in water to which mustard had been added. The water temperature was increased until I was par-boiled, then put to bed with heaps of blankets.

More enjoyable to me, there being no bathroom, I was bathed in the copper in the scullery. This was of course on Monday after the washing was finished. Wash day was a business – clothes were boiled in the copper, a brick affair heated by a little fire underneath. The clothes were then dumped in the dolly tub, soap and blue bag added, then mother walloped it around with the dolly. Then came the mangling to squeeze out the water. This was such hard work that Dad stayed home until the mangling was finished.

A so well-remembered shop was the cobblers. It could hardly be described as a shop – just a tiny crowded room in a little two-storey building reached from Tap Road. The only lighting was a small window looking out over the Dom. There, surrounded by boots and shoes and pieces of strong leather and wax, Mr Greatorex hammered away on his last. He peered over his glasses when we entered the shop. There was no greeting beyond a grunt; his lips held a row of rivets ready to be driven into the shoe he was repairing. He was a great friend of Dad's. He frequently called on him on his way from work.

A few yards further towards the Market Place Harry Swift the pork butcher was very busy. He sold all manner of porky products. Bacon, hams, chops, pigs' feet, lard stored in pigs' bladders, black pudding, pigs feet, chicklings, etc. Dad used to say "if they could catch the pig's whistle they would sell it". Harry Swift, of course, killed his own pigs. Sometimes we would hang over his gate to watch. Some of the boys begged the pig's bladder which, inflated, gave us a kind of ball to chase after.

Harry's son, another Harry, not a happy man who looked very sour, every day had to feed the pigs in the sty behind North Street. He carried the swill in two pails which hung from a yoke across his shoulders. He wore black leather gaiters. Dad too had a pair which he wore occasionally.

I had almost forgotten the Co-op. Mother took me there occasionally – a bit low in the social scale where "divi" was allowed on all purchases. It was the smell of oranges that reminds me of it. Tomatoes were packed in brown dust, it might have been peat or coconut fibre. The floor was covered in sawdust

The butcher's shop was another shop which was carpeted with sawdust. I suppose I was a little older when I went to buy meat, always sirloin. Mother would instruct me to ask for 4lbs weight or four shillings worth whichever gave the right amount. Mr Snow in his blue and white striped apron served me, stuffing the money into his pockets, there was no till. His back pocket bulged with notes. I picked up a ten shilling note that had escaped. I don't think he would have missed it – equivalent to 10 bobs worth of prime beef.

Mr Botham, a man with a deep voice, kept the fish shop in the Market Place. He sang in the Chapel choir. He also sold vegetables. The fish scrap waste and the cabbage leaves he used to dig into his little garden alongside Water Lane.

Two trades which we loved to watch; one, the blacksmith Billy Mee. Unlike the traditional figure of a smith, big and brawny with a beard and ruddy complexion, Billy, though very tough, was tallish but thin and with little colour. Horses came to be shod. There was a wonderful smell and a great hissing when the hot shoe, straight from the fire, was placed on the horses hoof. The horse quietly munched at a bag of oats strung round his head and appeared unconcerned.

The other trade was that of the wheelwright. His work yard was overlooked from the Prom. He frequently had to fix a new iron rim on a cartwheel, after repair of spokes or hub. The wheel was lain flat on the ground and blocks placed under the wooden rim. The new rim had been made slightly less in circumference than the wooden wheel. The wood was burned, but before any damage could be done, the iron rim was cooled by buckets of water being thrown over it. The iron rim now fitted tightly in place.

Thinking back to the chemist, for much of the needs of the village for slight accidents or perhaps not so slight illnesses this was the first service. Doctors had to be paid. I was carted off to see the doctor after falling out of a tree. Behind Scarthin there is a ridge; it used to be wooded and was a favourite playground. In a clearing was the judgment tree, or so it was called. It had a short thick trunk with branches spreading outwards within easy reach of our short legs. There we would sit. As I said I fell off it cutting my hand quite badly. I still have this scar. I am sure we have all in a daft moment had our fortune told from our palm. On two occasions, the fortune tellers have abruptly terminated the interview when tracing the life line and had found it to be slashed across. They assumed that my existence would be curtailed.

Childhood Days in Cromford

Illness was common amongst the children I played with. Some of the parents were entirely dependent on the Mill for work. Temporary stoppages, short time were common enough. Housing in Scarthin was very poor. I so well remember going into one; it was, I think, a sort of basement to an old chapel. It was dark, the smell was appalling, it must have been penetrated by the drainage from the hovels immediately behind and above on the steep slope.

Measles, mumps, scarlet fever, were regularly visited on us. We had awful teeth. I was plagued by styes and impetigo, a horrid scabby infection. (Styes had to be rubbed with a gold wedding ring to help them to burst!) Periodically the nurse came into the school. She unfortunately was always referred to as the "nit nurse". Yes, nits were shared by all of us. Mother had a special comb to mount her campaign against my infestation. The nurse's responsibility was to check our general development, testing hearing and checking sight and teeth. Following one of these examinations I was taken to a clinic in Matlock where five milk teeth and two bits were extracted. No fuss, just pulled out.

We went to school one morning to learn that little Jimmy, one of a small tribe of Greenoughs, had died. Parents who could afford tried to insure against this all too common occurence by taking out small policies. Mother was one of these. The insurance man used to call; I remember him so well with his dark suit, his pen which he dipped in a little glass inkpot which he magically produced from his waistcoat pocket. The scheme was for a penny a week, a policy which we carried on for years after we were married having almost forgotten what it was for. The insurance company, the 'Pru', eventually bought it out and even then it was only valued at a few pounds.

What did we wear? How were we clothed? The children all had shoes or boots. Rarely did we see bare feet, but for boys many were 'ragged-arsed'. Where families were large the brothers were always in the process of growing out of, or growing into trousers. Father's cast-offs frequently covered the whole family. But dressed for school we wore short trousers, stockings held up by garters, a woollen jersey and always a tie. Caps were small versions of the flat caps worn by adults.

CHAPTER THREE

SHALL WE HAVE AN EGG FOR TEA?

Shall we have an egg for tea?

I was about seven years old when we left Scarthin House to move to a little cottage high up on Cromford Hill, one of many built by Sir Richard Arkwright to house the workers in his mill.

Some months before we were due to leave, Dad had bought a barn in Water Lane on the opposite side of the Cromford Dam, in order that he could continue trading. The barn, stone built, had a loft running the full length of the building made accessible by means of an open wooden stairway. The entrance was by a heavy sliding door which when closed could be secured by a padlock.

To improve the premises Dad made a wood and glass shop front, retaining the sliding door. The floor was cobbled, very rough, very dirty, so all was concreted over. With the installation of electric lighting and a coke stove, the transformation was almost complete, but not before he made a shop sign in wooden lettering screwed to the sliding door – "George Allsop Cabinet Maker and French Polisher". He was now in business.

Some time later with a view to living nearby he bought from Mr Snow, a butcher, the small field behind the shop. Mr Snow had set up a chicken house next to an old pigsty long disused. Why not keep a few hens?

Soon the first occupants took up residence, a family with varied pedigrees – a pair of White Leghorns, a pair of Black Leghorns, rather nervous flighty birds likely to take to the air if disturbed. These were joined by a pair of Buff Orpingtons, sedate well-feathered creatures with low slung chassis. Finally a magnificent Rhode Island Red Cockerel who surveyed his new estate, particularly his residents, with an air of disdain.

The hens soon settled down and began to pay their keep. The white hens laid white eggs, the buff coloured ladies produced brown eggs, but what of the black? An old riddle. All this of course without any reference to their lord. This state of affairs could not be tolerated, so the pecking order must be established and observed. The wives who regularly produced eggs were invited to share the lord's table. Having found some tasty morsel the select few pecked away happily under his approving eye. Those however failing to reach the expected standards were chivied around unmercifully.

Now we had eggs in plenty and to spare, but the field was large, the accommodation commodious. Do we buy more birds? Why should we? Dad put together a small hen-box up in the loft with a little netting, and a broody hen was presented with a clutch of new eggs to hatch and left to get on with it. In so very few days she proudly presented us with a family of tiny yellow chicks, far too small to face the rough and tumble of the great world outside. Dad extended the wire enclosure and the chicks grew rapidly, creatures with stubby wings, long skinny necks, making a fearful clamour at feeding time.

Naturally some were young cockerels and, along with the pullets, went to join the favoured few. Old Rhodie accepted the increase to his harem with splendid indifference, but let one of the young bloods try his chance! R.I.R.s comb, already fiery red, would glow, almost steam, his eye menacing, then if threats had failed he would rush headdown, wings flapping in a cloud of dust to rout the intruder. Dad would eye such goings on as unacceptable in the little kingdom he had created. No problem – one for the pot.

And so the day would end peacefully. Old Rhodie would, almost on the dot at four-o-clock, lead his extended family down to the stile opposite the shop door to remind Dad that it was time for tea.

CHAPTER FOUR

CROMFORD SCHOOL
1923–1929

Sir Richard Arkwright the industrialist needed housing for his workers and to this end built much of the Cromford we see today. Rows of small cottages, in groups, separated only by the passageways giving access to the rear. From the Market Place to high on Cromford Hill they front the road on one side only, but the pattern is broken by a single street, North Street, where the cottages face one another across the road. At the end is Cromford School.

Cromford School consisted of one large room, divided by a ceiling-high wooden partition with glass panes so that all classes could be overlooked.

I first became a pupil there in 1923. The teaching staff at that time were:-

Headmaster, Mr H Daniels,
Miss Cardin, senior mistress who taught the 7–8 year olds,
Miss Limb responsible for the infants,
Miss Dickenson, groups aged 9–10
At age eleven boys and girls were taught by Mr Daniels.

From my first day I was in the care of Miss Limb, a kind gentle soul, well liked by the infants. I was given a slate and slate pencil and instructed to copy the letters on the blackboard. Our work inspected we were told to wipe it off and try again. We each had a small wet rag for this purpose. As I had learned to read and write at home I was allowed to have a pencil and paper.

Other than the daily dose of the 3 R's we did spend some time on handicrafts. We were presented with a circular piece of cardboard with a hole in the middle. By passing strands of raffia through the hole and over the edge and back again we produced quite adequate tablemats. For the skilled, another version was produced by threading the raffia through a needle and wrapping the thread round a few strands of raffia to make a button and then by stitching and wrapping a coil would grow quite quickly to form a most beautiful mat.

We also attempted modelling figures with plasticene. The material we were given was once in the form of brightly coloured bars, but now a uniformly dirty grey colour. However by squeezing, pressing and twisting in our grubby little hands we created fantastic forms and were happy with the result. Similarly, coloured chalks had also deteriorated, pieces long enough to be used had to be scrabbled for amidst the dust and gravel.

There were two playgrounds laid one above the other on the sloping ground. The surface was, I think, limestone grit, hard on the knees. We infants had the use of the lower playground, where unfortunately we were at the mercy of the boys on the higher level who in winter following snow would bombard us with snowballs. Playtime ended when Miss Cardin emerged to wield her large brass bell. The squealing and shouting ceased abruptly and we filed quietly into our classrooms.

Came the end of my first term and Christmas was near. On the last day of term our two teachers had contrived to produce a Christmas Tree which we decorated with bits of silver paper and ribbon, and, wonder of wonders there was an iced cake made by Miss Carding. We were each given a small piece wrapped in paper to take home. Sadly I left mine in the cloakroom.

I think I was about seven years old when I moved into Miss Dickenson's class, a teacher with red-gold hair and a sharp tongue. By this time we were reading and writing quite well and could do simple sums. And of course, tables; it was surprising how quickly we learned them, chanting them all together at school and then quietly at home. Without this basic knowledge in no way could we have coped with the standard of arithmetic we should be expected to have when we moved up into the big school.

But for now we had singing lessons based on the Sol-Fah system. Whilst Miss Dickenson taught the girls to sew Mr Daniels instructed the boys in the first elements of drawing, a basic skill which has stood me in good stead.

Eventually I moved into the big school and was to learn long division and multiplication, highest common factor, lowest common denominator, even square roots and then decimals, and what at the time seemed so inappropriate for children of millworkers, stocks and shares. For English we were given short lists of words to learn to pronounce and spell and on which we would be tested after the lunch break; words such as antirrhinum, rhododendron, words which, even now, make me consult a dictionary.

I particularly enjoyed the geography classes which included a little geology. During his long headship Mr Daniels had accumulated an impressive collection of minerals and fossils gathered from many visits to the quarries and old leadmines in the area. Part of this collection was displayed in a large glass-fronted cabinet. I was given to understand that he was in the habit of rewarding scholars who brought him interesting specimens. It is to Gaffer Daniels that I owe my life-long interest in geology.

A strict disciplinarian, handy with the cane, punishment deserved, never administered harshly, Mr Daniels earned our respect. On one celebrated occasion Mr Key, who had property nearby, complained that boys had been seen hurling sticks up into his walnut tree in order to dislodge the unripe fruit. It did not need Mr Sherlock Holmes to unmask the offenders. The boys were lined up, hands outstretched – walnut stained fingers! – conclusive evidence – punishment administered – case file closed.

We sat goggle-eyed one day; a girl had brought in a glass of water in which twisted and turned a threadworm* that had appeared from their water tap. Mr Daniels measured it, wrote the details on a postcard, and I suppose posted it on to the appropriate authority.

There is on Cromford Moor a lane which we knew as Alaba Lane. From the map it is named Alabaster Lane. As there are no gypsum deposits in our part of Derbyshire it can be assumed that alabaster was once worked there. In Matlock Bath Museum there are numerous items turned from this material. In our school the older boys were taught by the headmaster to work alabaster on

*Threadworm – any of various parasitic threadlike nematode worms.
Concise Oxford Dictionary

Cromford School 1923–1929

CYRIL JIM ? OSSIE JOE ARTHUR FRED FRANK TOP
HODGKINSON SHAW * WORTHY ALLSOP RUSSELL MILLWARD BROWN ROW

ELSIE LILY KATHLEEN REBBIE LIZZIE ? EVELYN ? SARAH SECOND
GREATOREX HODGKINSON HOLMES BOND BOWN * DITCHFIELD * MOUNTAIN ROW

MISS LIMB DAPHNE KATHLEEN EILEEN ? WINNIE ? EVELYN JOYCE THIRD
TEACHER SMEDLEY FLETCHER CAULOW * BEST * BUNTING WHITWORTH ROW

ADA ANNIE LUCY KEN CONNIE EILEEN LIZZIE FOURTH
BRAILSFORD BROWN PORTER WILD MARSDEN BRITLAND BUCKLEY ROW

STAN HARRY ARTHUR WALTER GEORGE HAROLD EDDIE BOTTOM
PIDCOCK HOLMES HOLMES MOTTERSHED PIDCOCK BROOKS ALLSOP ROW

Cromford School Infants, with Miss Limb, 1926 (or 1924?).

lathes constructed entirely of wood and driven by foot pedals. In theory small vases or dishes could be made but this required some patience. The lathes could be pedalled at great speed causing the most awful racket much to the annoyance of Miss Dickenson who was trying to teach sewing to the girls. Unfortunately the embryo vase would be smashed earning the wrath of Gaffer Daniels who applied the cane quite liberally. Miss Cardin's father lived in Matlock Bath and I believe he might have been involved in this craft; he certainly supplied the raw material to the school.

Also for the boys there was the school garden behind the cottages in North Street adjoining the school. This, I understand, was a much more successful enterprise. Beyond being given a rake to hold I do not remember contributing very much to its success.

On Oak Apple Day, thought to commemorate a certain monarch who had evaded the Commonwealth troops by hiding up an oak tree, the boys guarded the school entrance brandishing nettles with which they attacked the bare legs of anyone not having a sprig of oak leaves pinned to their clothes.

Perhaps I should have stated earlier in this narrative that our school was in the care of the Church of England represented by Canon Hazlehurst who visited us occasionally to make sure that we were having religious instruction. Each day school began with a prayer and a hymn. The hymns were printed on sheets of oilcloth linked together to form a huge swatch which hung high above our heads. In Lent Canon Hazlehurst led us through the churchyard to St. Mark's Church (since demolished). There we had to sit or kneel making suitable responses to the Litany. The church was unheated, damp, musty and cold. Verily we were miserable little sinners!

A very few Minor Scholarships were awarded giving admission to the Ernest Bailey Grammar School at Matlock. Likewise a few free places were available which were taken up at the Anthony Gell Grammar School in Wirksworth. I was fortunate to gain entrance to Matlock and it was whilst I was a scholar there that Headmaster Daniels came up to retirement age. The ceremony was conducted at Cromford School in the presence of Canon Hazelhurst, the school governors and many former pupils. Mr Daniels must have been a proud fulfilled man, that it should be a former pupil, once a Cromford man, now headmaster of the Ernest Bailey Grammar School, Dr. Chapman, who made the presentation.

For many years after she retired into a house overlooking the Cromford Dam and Scarthin, Miss Cardin, each evening, would step out to the front of her home to ring a curfew on her handbell, to remind all the generations of children that she had taught that, in her judgement, it was time that they were off the streets and off to bed.

CHAPTER FIVE

THE BARBER

a more important customer

To most of my generation 'Chivers' spelt jars of preservatives, a guarantee of the quality of the jams and marmalades they sold in huge quantities. To me it is a Mr Chivers who brings back so clearly the memory of a building at the junction of the A6 and the Lea and Wirksworth roads. At Cromford Tors, isolated from the village, stood this odd little building, perhaps octagonal in shape, but constructed entirely of wood, the main frame members picked out in black, the panels and window frames in white.

Here in his own little world Mr Chivers plied his trade – he was the village barber. In his shop we sat on wooden benches all facing inwards allowing us to admire the skill and dexterity of our barber as great wadges of hair fell from heads revealing cranial contours that had not seen the light of day for weeks.

Shelves, high on the walls, carried mugs each with a name painted on it, and each containing soap and a shaving brush. These were the property of customers who preferred to employ a barber, many of whom, it has to be said, allowed their whiskers to grow until the weekend. Saturday was sprucing-up-day when a man should look his best whether for a pint and a game of dominoes at the Boat Inn, or the football match in Derby, or, attired in his navy blue serge suit, he would be fit to escort his wife who might want to show off her fox-fur looped around her neck in church. Mother had such an ornament; she would lay it on the seat beside me and during the sermon I would play with the beady-eyed muzzle at one end and stroke the brush at the other. I digress.

I was one who sat in Mr Chiver's shop on Saturday mornings for my turn and to watch and wait and fidget for what seemed an eternity. At last I would be called forward to kneel on a wooden stool with a cloth draped around my small person. Mr Chivers was tall and disliked stooping to work. This practice of requiring boys to kneel was eventually banned, but not in my time. A number of children had knelt so long that they had fainted and fallen off the stool. Apparently they had been temporarily abandoned to make way for a more important customer. My present hairdresser uses a slab of wood upholstered in black leatherette which he lays across the arms of the barber's chair. The child is lifted up and placed on this seat. How's that for modernisation?

As a boy, amazingly, I was offered a choice of hairstyles. I could choose the twopenny all off, which allowed Mr Chivers to make a clean sweep with his hand-operated clipper, except that fashion demanded that a little quiff should remain which somehow added an extra look of surprise to the innocent face. Not for me – I can't remember whether I offered a threepenny bit or whether I was especially selected because my neck was clean, but I did have a mop of wavy black hair, so I had a carefully contrived haircut that would meet Mother's inspection and approval.

Poor Mr Chivers. He was a pale, thin, sad-looking man with a little cough. When he needed to cough, and this was very frequently, he would turn away and politely cough into his fist. Nevertheless he always joined in the cheerful chatter and village gossip. Inevitably, of course, he died of consumption. I have no idea whether anyone carried on the business after his passing, but I do know that the little building has been a tea shop. No, I have not forgotten Mr Chivers.

CHAPTER SIX

GOING TO THE PICTURES

In my early days we went occasionally to the "pictures". No such word as "cinema" had been written into the language. Our little share of this wonderful make-believe world was played out in the "Kursaal"* by the Fish Pond in Matlock Bath. This building has always been everything and nothing to Matlock Bath. No venture, theatre, dance hall, picture-house has lasted more than a year or two. Now known as the Pavilion it is currently being used as a museum of mining. When Matlock Bath was a spa the waters could be taken in the Pump Room and it is still possible to sample the mineral water there to this day. But always the huge cost of keeping the building maintained to meet the demands of modern standards is well nigh impossible.

But to return to the pictures. The main hall to me was huge and the floor was level for dancing. The screen was erected on a huge stage. There was always a lot of noise, seats were just chairs, no upholstery to absorb the noise. In the corner below the stage on the right, stood a piano. A friend of ours, Mrs Brookes, played for the show. I haven't the faintest idea how she found music to accompany the film, but the general rule seemed to be that during quiet scenes unintrusive music was required, but as the action being portrayed became more exciting, the tension mounting, Mrs Brookes played faster and louder. Of course we were all on the edge of our seats. Occasionally, however, Dad deemed that some of the play was not for my impressionable eyes and would stretch out an arm to hide me from these excesses.

The management of the Picture House would add to the drama. The "Blue Danube" I think it was, was being shown. At a convenient

---

*Kursaal – a building for the use of visitors at a health resort, esp. at a German spa.

moment a suitable slide was slipped in, the action temporarily halted, and a spotlight was focussed on a figure in evening dress complete with starched shirt and dicky bow. With the piano for accompaniment he rendered a suitable song. All the time, of course, we gazed hopefully at the screen which would signal the end of the interruption. As this could happen two or three times during the show, I, at least, was completely bored.

Bearing in mind that colour film was way, way off in the future, imagine the excitement when a red slide was introduced to give reality to a great fire. Everything and everyone in the hall became a deep pink. For a battle scene the management really excelled themselves – fireworks were let off, somebody banged a drum, Mrs Brookes produced crashing chords; the smoke and the smell of gunpowder all brought the feeling that we were having our money's worth.

For me, however, perhaps I got more than my money's worth when I was taken to see "Four Horsemen of the Apocalypse". I was scared stiff when they appeared to ride towards me. I suffered nightmares for ages after. Happily the main event was always preceded by a comic film. Cops and robbers rushed about, their antics producing howls of laughter. Cartoons were very popular; "Felix the Cat" was favourite; Mickey Mouse had not been invented I think. But we all used to sing or chant

"Felix keeps on walking, keeps on walking still,
with his tail behind him, you will always find him!"

CHAPTER SEVEN

ONE SUNDAY MORNING

It has been a disappointing spring, heavy rain, cold winds have beset us; but today perhaps the weather has at last changed for the better. This morning has dawned with all that we could wish for, a brilliant blue sky with a few fluffy clouds that will soon burn away in the warm sunshine, and a soft gentle breeze.

It is Sunday morning and scarcely a sound disturbs the quiet. The dawn chorus which woke us early with its joyful clamour is over, the birds have settled down to rest after their first quest for food. In a very few days they will have young nestlings to feed and then there will be no rest from dawn to dusk.

On the Cromford Dam the silence is broken only by the moorhens and dippers quarrelling with Mrs Pidcock's ducks who live just under the wall. The swans have a half-built nest almost in the middle of the pond, but will they complete it? Rarely do they raise a family [as rarely did "Joey" and his partner in the 1970's and 80's . . . DJM].

The mills are closed, only the maintenance men will be at work ensuring that the machines will be ready to work at full capacity come Monday morning. The overshot wheel by our little mill is still, only the splash of water escaping the sluice can be heard.

Even on Sundays some must work. Up on Cromford Moor the farmers have been up early as on every other day to feed their stock, the cows have to be milked then turned out on to the green pastures. Strangely though, the chickens are kept in the coops, the young ponies remain in the stables. For hundreds of years this land was torn apart in the quest for lead ore, now the grass grows green over the old tips. On such a morning as this there is a heavy dew which somehow is contaminated by lead absorbed and carried up on to the leaves of the grass. Until the sun dries the grass, this 'belland' the name by which it is known, is dangerous to young animals. Presumably in wet weather it is washed away.

Smoke rises from the chimneys of some of the cottages across in Scarthin drifting lazily in the warm sunshine. Fires are being built up to heat the side-ovens of the black-leaded grates. Wives are preparing the Sunday roast that will supply most of the main meals of the following week, taken hot, sliced cold, reheated with an oxo cube thrown in, lastly chopped into small pieces served with potato-hash!

High on the hillside someone has opened his pigeon-loft, the birds rise up quickly, swirl around, grouping, then down again, only to lift off for further circuits. They must build up their strength; in a few days some of them will be put into wicker baskets, taken down to Cromford Station, loaded carefully into the guards van of a slow train and carried far away to be released again to fly home to that small black and white striped hut in Scarthin.

The doors of the Wesleyan Chapel are flung wide, the first of the worshippers are entering in their twos and threes having a few words with the steward and then inside finding their accustomed seats, mostly preferring the sides or near the back, few march down to the front.

No ancient gnarled oak pews here; the seats are of soft pine polished to give a rich reddish-brown hue. Some seat backs have been revarnished as part of the spring clean. On the communion table are vases of daffodils and tulips arranged by Mother, whose turn it was to 'do the flowers'.

Mrs Wright, our organist, is arranging her music and finding the first hymn chosen for the service. Suddenly there is a rustle of excitement; the visitors from Willersley Castle are crowding in. They are to share morning prayer with us. The Castle has been acquired by the Methodist Guild as a place for holidays and many of the guilders led by Mr Mutton the manager have walked down the drive from the Castle over the ancient bridge to turn in by St. Marys Church following the lovely Church Walks by the river to the Tors. They are a happy crowd; the ladies in floral dresses or costumes, the men, some wearing coloured suits, have button-holes and name tags pinned to their lapels.

Mrs Wright starts her first voluntary. The organ is old and has to be nursed. It is advisable not to use the pedalboard during quiet passages as they tend to rattle. Alas the organ is hand blown, the bellows wheezy, the blower arm long and heavy. A little weight on the console indicates whether the bellows are full, a corresponding weight behind the organ has to be very carefully watched as the music being played may call for many stops to be opened, the pressure falls dramatically, the musical output is reduced to a dreadful wail, calling for desperate pumping with some bumping.

Our choir will not, for once, feel under any kind of pressure to lead the singing; often enough with a small congregation scattered around a fairly large building we have to make a great effort. We are fortunate in having Miss May Adkin, a lady with a wonderful soprano voice, Mr Botham the greengrocer who sings bass, a basso-profundo indeed, Alf Wright and his wife Phyllis, Miss Cissie Tomlinson in millinery, Les Wright, gentleman's outfitter, the Dickensons and Morton the plumber. We all lend support. I suppose we number ten, about fifteen on a good day.

> *"Praise my soul the King of Heaven*
> *To his feet thy tribute bring;*
> *Ransomed, healed, restored, forgiven,*
> *Who like me his praise should sing?*
> *Alleluia! Alleluia! Praise the everlasting King".*

The first hymn is sung, full throated, everyone knows the words; we learned them as small children, scarcely a need for hymn books. The lessons read, the offertory taken – what a pleasant sound the tinkle of coins can produce on the plates as they are passed around. Oh sordid thought! – there should be a small improvement in our church finances. It is very warm, the chapel doors have been left open; we will not be disturbed by traffic.

Our guests have brought their host with them, a genial man well known in the sports world – he is to deliver the sermon. We settle back in our seats in pleasant anticipation that we are to be entertained. Entertained in Chapel? It will be a welcome change for us; our local preachers, bless them, cannot help but remind us of the evils of strong drink and the hell and damnation that awaits the sinners. Already we have fallen under the speaker's spell, alternately serious and then bringing smiles even to some of our more staid whose faces rarely exhibit more than a contagious gloom.

The final hymn is announced, and we all rise to our feet, but horror of horrors, because of the day's heat and the close contact with warm bodies, the new varnish has become tacky. Flowery dresses are tending to adhere to the seats. Fortunately there is no tearing, but the pretty fabrics have left their imprint in the form of fine fibres.

Our visitors took their leave of us with little complaint, but for all that we were considerably embarrassed. As one of our stalwarts might have said "A reckon as 'ow we'll ha' t' spend some o' that there money on them tha' pews. We munna 'ave owt like that 'appen agen."

It is quite probable that next Sunday Mr Mutton will lead his flock down through the Castle grounds to the River Derwent to walk up stream following the path into Lovers' Walks, there to cross over the Jubilee Bridge to swell the congregation in the Methodist Chapel in Matlock Bath. It is equally probable that the holiday-makers might come again to Cromford?

There was a hurried meeting of the elders. The varnish would have to be cleaned off before next Sunday. It fell to my father, George Allsop, a cabinetmaker and french polisher, whose shop was next door to the Chapel, to scrape and sand away the sticky varnish. This accomplished, he enquired from the elders how they would like the works completed. Unfortunately they could not agree as to whether the new varnish could be safe to sit on before the next morning service. As week followed week, they could not make up their minds. The bared wood remained unadorned.

CHAPTER EIGHT

THE WAKES

The event that for a few short days changed Cromford from being a quiet, peaceful village to a centre of colour, noise and a positive riot of unbelievable delights was the coming of the Wakes. It was on Sunday evening when Henry Hall and his fair assembled in Cromford Meadows and there the trucks, vans and caravans had to wait until after seven o'clock when it was adjudged the Church service was over. We ran to the Market Place where the fair would be created from the strange panels, poles and tents carried on the wagons. To our eyes the most astonishing vehicles were the great

Carnival Queen and attendants (date? before the War) from the left: Nellie Redfern, Pearl Wild, Pearl's sister, Ellen Holmes, Miss Bunting.

steam traction engines, one of which was named "Lord Curzon" (after the Viceroy of India). These tractors provided the motive power and lighting for the roundabouts, shaking, thundering and creating a lovely cloud of oily steam. The side stalls were lit by naptha flares which in the wind appeared to threaten the very stalls to which they were attached.

The greatest attraction was "the Whales" comprising carriages in green, red and gold with huge, open jaws at the front and a curled tail at the rear. In motion they rose and plunged as in a stormy sea, all the time being heralded by a steam organ tended by King Neptune and his Sea Nymphs. I loved to ride on this machine. The Carousel with its galloping horses and shining brass poles to which we clung, scared me as I feared being thrown off. The steam organ on this machine played the 'pops' of the period.

To further mark the occasion there followed on the Saturday a carnival, the whole village and surrounding communities contributed to make this a memorable occasion. Sunday evening brought the series of events to its conclusion. The roundabouts were still and silent, but it was here that Middleton Silver Band gave a concert and last of all accompanied the audience in a hymn. Canon Hazlehurst gave the blessing and it was all over for another year. By Monday morning Henry Hall and his fair had vanished as if it had never been.

CHAPTER NINE

A JOB AT 'MILL

Mr John Marsden-Smedley.

My father was very angry. I was leaving school. He had been to discuss my future with the Headmaster of Ernest Bailey Grammar School, Mr Orme. I had not done too badly, so I thought, but apparently failed to impress him. He suggested that a vacancy should be sought in a good garage. "What, after all these years' education?" Dad would have none of it. I know now how sound was the advice Mr Orme offered.

Shortly after, one morning bright and early, I cycled the two miles to Lea Mills to join the white collared, with a little corner, a little stool to perch on, to be at the beck and call of all and sundry.

One of my first tasks was to type labels to be stuck under appropriate bells; one I printed "Miss Booth", the other "Edward". They reappeared as "Secretary" and "Office Boy". From then, my position in the pecking order having been established, I was soon to learn that "Where's that boy?" meant me.

A few steps up from the street door, a small area of cork lino and brown painted woodwork; on the left, the enquiry office with a telephone switchboard. High on a shelf stood blue gloss fire extinguishers that oozed some white substance and beneath, fire buckets filled with sand. On entry the eye immediately focussed on a great clock of polished steel and brass safely esconced in a glass cabinet, a clock that was to slowly tick away the hours which I was to spend in this office.

An office, small by any standard, this was the headquarters, the base of power of one of the leaders in the hosiery industry, John Smedley & Sons. The little offices accommodated the Chairman, John Marsden Smedley, his son Jack, together with Mr Nieper and Mr Fred Ollerenshaw. The chairman was a very tall, quite slimly built man who moved surprisingly quickly, but in shambling fashion and scared everyone as he would charge out of his office shouting for attention.

I was allocated a place in the enquiry office. The telephone switchboard, similar to those in any telephone exchange was operated by Mary Lowe. I was expected to stand in for her during meal breaks and so quickly learned to operate it myself. It has to be said that I must have severely tested the patience of the operator at the Matlock exchange, who in order to speed up transmission of telegraphed orders, telephoned them directly, confirmation being received the following day by the postman.

There was yet another door, a door which was a mystery to me, through which passed men and girls, never casually, always hurriedly as if their very presence in this office invited censure. I was one day to be transferred to the factory office. Through that door was a noisy, smelly, steamy world of clanking, roaring, hissing machinery tended by girls, hair tied up in cloths, men shirt-sleeved, people who I learned to admire and respect as I gradually got to know them.

In order to reach the factory the way led through what must have been the oldest buildings of a mill sited astride a little tributary of the River Derwent, which, flowing down the valley, served first the Cupolas, an old lead smelting works and then was caught up in a dam which had once powered the mill. Now steam and electricity had transformed a small business into a comparatively large enterprise. The various processes of turning raw wool into yarn took place in rooms at all levels, seemingly built higgedly-piggedly on a steeply sloping site.

In one of the deepest darkest areas, raw wool from huge bales was being passed through carding machines, machines designed to straighten out the fibres, a process once carried out using teazles by families in their own homes. The wool emerged from the carder as a long loose filament coiling snake-like into tall drums.

A Job at 'Mill

In another room women, surely the lowest paid, turned wooden wheels three feet in diameter, winding hanks on to bobbins. In the spinning room spindles of tightly wound yarn awaited further processing, but in the mule room girls and men tended great machines, part of which rolled outwards over the floor, all the time doubling and twisting yarns to be taken up on large cones as the machine went into reverse and retreated. The machinists followed walking forward, picking up, tying in loose ends of yarn, then allowing the machine to push them backwards, often sliding gently across a floor polished to glass by their feet. High overhead a huge steel cable running over pulleys alternately tightened and slackened threatening another Mr Ollerenshaw who stood at a little desk immediately beneath.

Another dark passage, a few worn wooden steps to climb, to be confronted by the factory door. Inside, the great floor, black with old oil, seemed to spread for ever, crowded as it was with rows and rows of knitting machines, hissing, clanking, hissing, clanking, each connected by leather belts connected to steel shafts high overhead but running quietly on smooth bearings. These machines were arranged in pairs facing each other with a narrow aisle between allowing one knitter to tend both. This was the production line where garment pieces, typically of vests and pants, were knitted, up to twelve at a time. Not only could straight fabric be prepared, but, under the hands of craftsmen, narrowings and widenings required for the fully fashioned knitwear of the high class hosiery market. All who have laboriously knitted small garments by hand know that occasionally the knitting needle slips out and all the stitches have to be picked up again. On these machines this is likely to happen whenever a change in the pattern being followed is made. Under its own weight the needle bar tends to roll backwards dropping all the stitches; on a twelve-head frame this can mean many hundreds! The machinist avoided this by controlled pressure on the hand-wheel, a large callous on the inside of the wrist was evidence indeed.

Ribs, cuffs and collars were knitted separately, then girls linked them to the body pieces. Most men of this period wore long johns, a very lucrative market. Smedley's invented a process in which the gusset was seamless; so successful was it that it was patented under

41

the name STARSEAT. The salesmen would demonstrate that two men hauling on a leg each could not tear them apart!

Other machines, patented by Jacquard, gave us lacy patterns, others ran off lengths for nightdresses, but the most fascinating of all gave not only lacework but overplating in colour. This standard of production called for carefully manufactured yarn, free from knots, and with an evenness of thickness and colour, otherwise the garment would be unsaleable.

Because of the incessant roar of the machinery it was virtually impossible to communicate except by close contact. On every frame was a safety guard, a steel plate covering the belt-driven driving pulley. Whenever Manager Mr Thompson popped out from his office, the first to spot him banged on his plate so warning all and sundry that he was about. However, when chairman John Marsden Smedley, Long John as he was known, appeared the same signal was passed but emphasised by a hand held high above the head, palm down.

On the whole the workforce carried out their duties cheerfully enough. Life was hard, hours long, Saturday morning attendance the norm. Buses collected girls from the surrounding villages, many from coalmining families around Alfreton, Clay Cross and Tibshelf. Others trudged miles, winter and summer, from Middleton and Bonsal. Opportunity for celebrations of engagements and weddings were always remembered, especially when the happy pair were both employed within the mill. This called for a mock wedding in which the reading of a long poem of many verses in the most bawdy language, humourous, embarrassing perhaps, good-hearted always, brought hoots and roars of laughter. Woe betide any man falling out of favour with the women. Of course there had to be initiation ceremonies for the fourteen year olds. Sooner or later, they would be seized, trousers removed, a liberal dressing of thick black grease applied or even a ring borrowed from a machine.

One snowy morning I arrived at work to find the office I worked in still locked, so off I went to borrow overseer Bunting's keys which he always left on the top of his desk, but, I forgot to return them. Mr Bunting, looking for them, decided that he must have left them at home. He had already had an horrendous journey from high on

Starkholmes hill, then sliding down Willersley Lane in his little car. Off he went and was gone some time being forced to walk back part of the way. He eventually discovered what had happened and swore quite comprehensively at me. His ire was somewhat tempered by the knowledge that everyone knew of his little adventure and were openly laughing at him. Our 'poet' wrote up the saga in many verses which was passed hand to hand. I wish now that I had a copy of it.

The wool store was under the factory floor, access obtained by a wooden ladder. Shelves stacked high, all carefully labelled, the weight of each parcel recorded, it was the duty of the storekeeper to ensure that he had a supply available to meet every demand. It was down here, safe from the management, that our barber earned a few pence.

On the way to the men's lavatories we had to pass the needle-maker's cabin, totally enclosed and dark with a little window through which we could watch him arrange bright new needles in a little block, then seal them in with molten lead. He was kept busy as needles were always twisted or broken. As I mentioned earlier the old factory was sited over a stream. Advantage was taken of this arrangement by building the lavatories projecting over the watercourse. They were horrible – the lime-washed walls adorned by obscene writings and names of previous occupants, perhaps the most memorable "A man's ambition must be small who writes his name on a shithouse wall". As there was a smoking ban throughout the factory it was to this place all came who needed a fag; a few who could not appease their craving for nicotine chewed tobacco, a special brand of which was available in any tobacconist.

Once the garments were completed, suitably ticketed for identification, the bundles were sent to be washed. The washhouse was surely the crudest imaginable plant – an arrangement of huge wooden paddles, suspended from a cam, slammed into the deep troughs of warm soapy(?) water, pummelling the woollens to remove the natural lanolin and swarf picked up from the various processes. A final clean wash and then they were sent to be stretched and steam-pressed, a transformation to a beautiful soft woollen. Only a last meticulous examination by the inspector and a Smedley's label stitched on before being packed into the distinctive, instantly recognisable, boxes bearing the Smedley Jay trademark.

Eddie Allsop, called up, 1939.

Inevitably fashion, particularly of outerwear, dictated production. The factory responded by introducing new designs, new colours. Nightdresses were knitted in a mixed yarn which included rayon giving a wonderful sheen to the delicate pastel colours. Those "messing about in boats" discovered seamen's jerseys and were envious. We gave them heavy navy-blue eleven-guage jerseys with huge roll collars in oiled wool that would last a lifetime.

A Job at 'Mill

Perhaps one development that really excited our imagination was the first bathing suit with separate bra and knickers, the gap "barely" one and a half inches, only acceptable in the Mediterranean, not even for bathers in Brighton!

An event that called for immediate reaction was the death of King George V. The court was ordered into strict mourning for six weeks. We were called on not only for black and white outerwear, but for a shade of purple reflecting, one supposes, the Royal Purple that was so rare and expensive that it was reserved for only the most high.

There has to be a downside. The vagaries of the fashion market affected those specifically engaged in producing outerwear; the main production of underwear, solid, reliable, was insulated. Orders for a new line that could be manufactured in a complete range of sizes and colours might dwindle to a half dozen, or even a quarter dozen. As the work force were paid wherever practicable by the piece, temporary suspensions were not infrequent.

My association with Smedley's Mill came unexpectedly to an end. It was on September 3rd 1939 that our Prime Minister, Mr Chamberlain, uttered his historic words which ended "Britain is now at war with Germany". During the following week I was called on to man the telephone switchboard in the late evening. I heard through the Matlock operator that a total blackout had been ordered. I passed the message on to the manager, Mr Thompson. Within minutes the evening shift came abruptly to an end. The factory, except for essencial maintenance staff was evacuated. The lights went out.

By the end of the week I was saying goodbye to the many friends I had made. I was the first, certainly not the last, to be called up for military service from the mill and just as I first rode on my bike for a job at 'mill I rode away for the last time.

APPENDIX 1

Recollections of the Business Life of Cromford in My Younger Days *by Jean Howsley*

This list was inspired by my 92-year-old Mother who was constantly asking "who lived in such-and-such a shop or house". Assisted by Eveline Fulwood and amidst much hilarity and "do you remembers" I set to and compiled this list. The final score stands at:–

67 businesses and shops of small tradesmen
3 public houses
2 bus companies
3 C of E churches
4 Chapels plus 1 RC (held in the Greyhound Yard)
We also had visiting travelling carts from other villages.

THE TOP OF THE HILL (commencing at Barnwell Lane)

Mr J Lomas	Farmer
Mr Taylor	Farmer and milkman
Mrs Bradley	Sweets and cigarettes
Mr Rollinson	Car Dealer
Mr S Taylor	Grocer
Mrs Taylor	Sweets (in house)
Miss M Mee	Grocer
Mr Young	Hardware
Mrs Wright	Grocer
Mr F Gibbs	Painter and Decorator
Mr Greatorex	Shoe Repairs
Mr T Robinson	Baker

Also a small laundry in Masons Opening and Mr Higton who bred and sold caged birds.

NORTH STREET

The Bell Inn	
Mr Priestley	Butcher
Mr Hine	Grocer
Mrs Slater	Sweets (in house)
Miss Barker	Dressmaker

BELOW NORTH STREET

Mr G Priestley	Electrical Engineer
Mr W Taylor	Joiner
J Swift & Sons	Wholesale tobacconists
Miss Kidd	Milliner and haberdashery
Misses H & E Essex	Dressmakers
Mr H Rolley	Joiner
Mr A Swift	Butcher
Mr J Sharples	Tailor
Mr M Gillott	Hairdresser

46

Mr J & H Kidd	Tinsmiths
Miss Smith	Newsagent
Mr C Kidd	Grocer
Mr J Newton	Post Office and Decorator
Mr J Gould	Draper

THE MARKET PLACE

Mr Mee	Blacksmith
Howards	Bakers, Grocers and Cafe
Walters & Brooker	Garage
Mr F Chapman	Draper
Mr F Chivers	Barber
Mr E Morten	Plumber
Mr R Botham	Greengrocer and Fishmonger
Mr T Boden	Shoeshop and Repairs (also sold ice-cream in summer)
Mr Slawson	Chemist
Mr E Wright	Tailor and Draper
The Greyhound Hotel	

WATER LANE

The Corner House had room for a part-time Dentist – a Mr Greatorex from Wirksworth

Mr Allsop	Furniture and Antiques
The Co-operative Stores	
Mr Bunting	Wheelwright and Undertaker
Miss Dawes	Piano lessons
Mr F Else	Garage and Haulage
Mr B Bond	Fish and chips

SCARTHIN

The Boat Inn	
Mr J Swift	Pork Butcher
Mr F Snow	Butcher
Mr S Britland	Grocer
Misses Kirk & Tomlinson	Hats and Drapery
W Smith & Co	Printers
Pidcock Bros	Bicycle shop
Mr Doxey	Baker
Mrs Dickinson	Sweets
Miss Woddwiss	Sweets
Mr Greatorex	Shoe repairs

MILL ROAD

Mr L Kay	Sweets and ice-cream
Offilers Brewery	
The Troy Laundry	
Wheatcrofts Coal Merchants	
Staffordshire Farmers (Corn Merchants)	
Railway Station	

APPENDIX 2

Our Local Lads (Cromford – 1915)

Our Country is at War, we wish it were not so
But it was forced upon us, so someone had to go;
Our lads were not behind, answering their Country's call
To go and fight for England, to either stand or fall.
We grieve to think that some have paid the price for glory great,
Their precious lives have given to save us Belgium's fate.
We think of Bonham Carter, Joe Tomlinson, Jack Brown,
Billy Sherrat and Bob Britland, whose lives have been laid down;
We grieve that Captain Arkwright met such a tragic fate,
for he was of the bravest, his loss to us is great;
We never shall forget them, these lads so brave and true
Who left our quiet village, their little bit to do;
Greater love hath no man – our loving Saviour said –
Than to give their lives for others; God rest our glorious dead.

We also think of brave Jim Holmes, who nobly took his part
To help to win the battle – the greatest ever fought,
And then there's Laurie Fryer who went early to the front
With our 'Little Contemptible Army' and bravely bore the brunt;
There's Jim Toplis, and Fred Holland, and Jimmy Gibbs as well,
Frank Brown, Joe Pidcock, George Gibbs, Sam Taylor too,
Along with Bert Parker, went their duty so to do;
Harry Britland and Geroge Lloyd, also Arthur Bidulph who
All were sent to the Dardanelles to try and break it through,
And then there's our brave Yeomanry who thought the Turks
    they'd try,
So they were sent to Egypt, then to Gallipoli –
Herbert Gillott and Tom Huddart, Alf Redfern and Fred Mee,
Wilfred Bosley, and Frank Fearn, and Owen Sudbury,
John Allan, and Tony Greatorex, along with Percy Wright.
And when they got to grips, showed how our Cromford lads
    could fight;
Then others of our local lads went into France 'somewhere'
To join our gallant Army and bravely do their share;
There's Mr Robinson's three sons – Harry, George and Tom,
They command the admiration, we feel sure of everyone.

There's George Ratcliffe and Sam Pearson, Harold Smith
    and Arthur Rose,
Dick Roberts and Jack Sherratt ready to meet all foes;
Then there's Tom and Harold Webster, Ernest Allen and
    John Gould,

Harry and Charlie Parker, all warriors brave and bold;
Jack Oldbury and Jack Vallance and Lewis Parker too
Belong to our brave Terriers who've gone their bit to do;
There's Jack Gregory, George Kirk, and also Tommy Fearn,
Laurie Newton and Tommy Dillon – all of our praises earn.
There's Fred Bunting come from Canada with the Princess Pats'
    to fight
It showed his heart was with us in this fight for truth and right.
Harry Pykett and Joe Sellors both joined the Veterinary Corps
To nurse our wounded horses they'll do their best we're sure.

We've still some left in England, training to use their guns,
And they'll not be found wanting when England needs her sons;
There's Will Waterfield, Willie Wright, George Byard and
    Fred Snow,
With Will Frith they'll be ready when Kitchener bids them go;
There's others we can think of, Laurie Musgrave and Percy Clay,
Arthur Siddall and Ernest Eaton all ready for the fray;
Joe Shaw, Tommy Britland, John Kidd and Willie Fearn,
Jim Botham and Joe Fearn, all doing their best to learn;
Will Holmes, Clifford Brooks, George Biddulph and Charlie White,
Wilfred Gregory and Joe Gladwin all went to join the fight;
There's Joe Wharton, George Pearson, Gus Smedley and
    George Blore,
And then there's Harry Kidd gone to join the Flying Corps;
Leonard Wilbraham, Willie Gould, Arthur Bunting and
    Maurice Kirk,
With Jack Allen and Willie Potter, their duty will not shirk.

What can we say of these brave lads who never thought of fear,
But left their homes and loved ones, and all that they held dear,
To go and fight for Britain the land of the brave and free,
To fight the cause of justice, of right and liberty.

We pray God to protect our lads and bring them safely through
That peace may quickly be restored is the wish of me and you;
And when the war is over and victory is won,
Cromford lads will share the honours in the great "well done".

All profits of the above to be given for Xmas boxes for local boys
Nov 19, 1915.